Dedicated to all hearts.

written and illustrated by Morgan Irby
text copyright 2024 by Morgan Irby
illustration copyright 2024 by Morgan Irby
www.morganashleyirby.com

# WHAT IS
# LOVE?
QUESTIONS FROM KIDS TO GOD.

BY: MORGAN IRBY

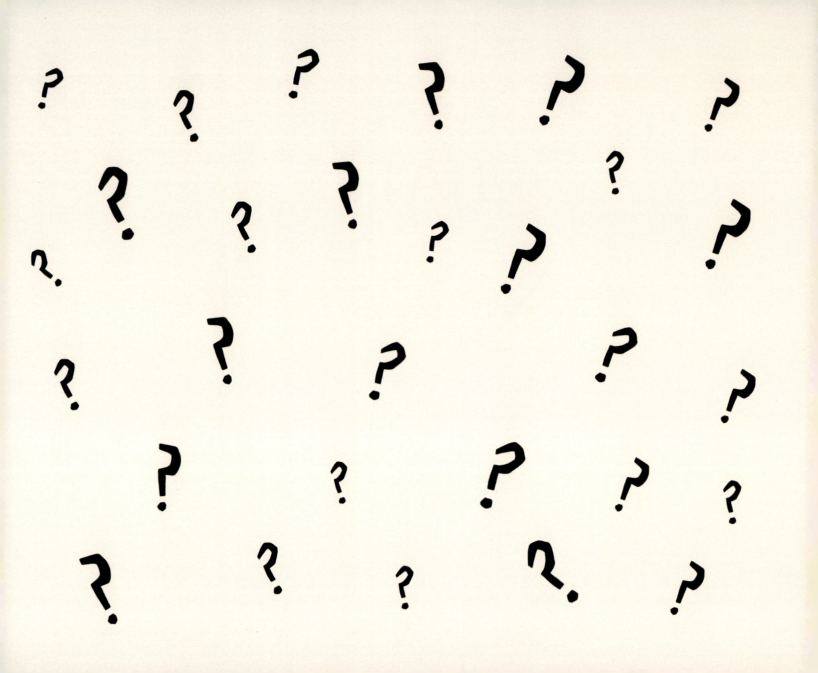

# WHAT IS LOVE?

The story is based on verses:
1 Corinthians 13:4-8
New International Version

4 Love is patient, love is kind. It does not envy, it does not boast, it is not proud. 5 It does not dishonor others, it is not self-seeking, it is not easily angered, it keeps no record of wrongs. 6 Love does not delight in evil but rejoices with the truth. 7 It always protects, always trusts, always hopes, always perseveres.
8 Love never fails.

"What is love and
how will we know?"
"I don't know!
What does it even look like?
Does it smell, does it grow?"

"WHOA! Let's take it slow
and figure this out as we go.
We'll ask the animals,
  they always have answers that humans don't know."

"We're on a search to define love, if you have time to spare, can you help us, Mr. Bear?"

"Oh yes, you've come to the right place. Hurry, there's no time to waste."

"Every year, bears like me, sleep to survive.
But no one gets jealous or tries to disturb my vibe!
God says, love is when we want the best for others
and as a bonus, we also feel good inside!"

"Even when we get honey,
we share it til there's nothing left!
God has taught us, love is not selfish...
when we give to others, we can all be blessed."

You get some honey

You get some honey

You get some honey

"Look, a blue jay, building its nest!"
"Hey, what is love?
How would you describe it best?"

I'm blue abba dee abba die

LOOK!!!  LOOK!!!

"And every season what begins as small twigs as these, eventually becomes my large home in the trees."

"What about badgers?
Do they know what love is?
I SEE ONE - HURRY!
Let's give them the love quiz!"

"WAIT, this could all go wrong.
The badgers don't like humans or bears,
we've known this for so long!

"You're such a funny fur ball!
God taught us not to dishonor others,
nor keep a record of your wrongs.
In fact, we weren't easily angered by the sight of you at all."

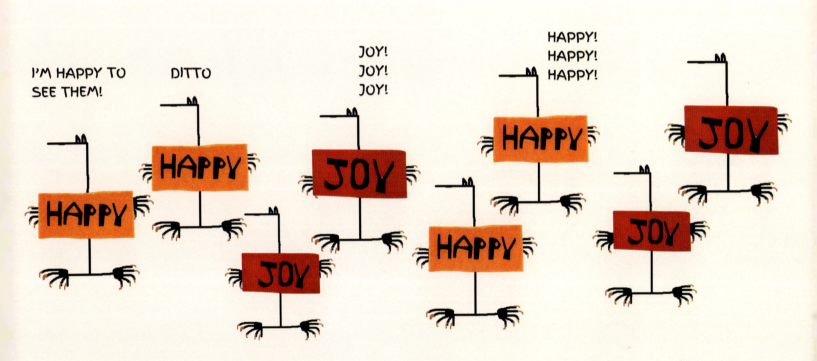

"Why don't we go talk with those frogs? Can you please tell us what you know about love, while you sit on your log?"

I think I lost a lash?

Bear has it!

"Well, aside from eating flies
and swimming all day,
we've learned that lying is not okay,
and it can hurt love in many ways."

"God said love rejoices in the truth,
that clarity is kind.
No matter how many frogs you have to kiss,
this is what you must wait to find."

LOVE

REJOICES

"Let's ask the horses a question before we go.
There's so much about love,
I bet they'll know!"

"All the animals look different,
some big, some small,
so tell us,
does love have anything to do
with looks at all?"

"Some animals brag about their good looks and believe it makes them better than most. But love has nothing to do with these things, God says it does not brag or boast."

"When it comes to your looks, please remember,
it is the least interesting thing about you by far,
love is not the way you look,
love is simply who you are."

"Oh no! I just realized, after all this talk, we're so far from the path!
And without a map, will we even be home in time for a bath?"

OH DE

"Look, I'm sorry to bother you, I just heard you are looking to define love. Do you mind if I tell you about it, as we soar from up above?"
"Uhhhhhhhhhhhh....yeah! Uhhhhhhhhhhhh....sure."

...YASSSSSS!!!

"Even though I'm known to build the biggest nests.
I'm not always there to keep my babies safe
from the most unwanted guests.
But I'm here to remind you, what God has taught me
through these difficult tests:

Love always protects, always trusts,
always perseveres.
And for y'all, even though your path home isn't clear,
God will make a way, he will keep you safe, my dears!

In fact, I will drop you off,
back where your journey began.
Back with Bear,
your trusted guide, your trusted friend."

"Bear, how can we ever repay you for your time?"

"That is the beauty of love, it is meant to be kind.
It was my pleasure, you do not owe me a dime."

IT'S ALL GOOD!
I'M HERE FOR YOU!

"Always remember...
love never fails
and the more you have,
the stronger you will grow.

Now it is up to you,
to share what you know,
to define love according to God's truth.
I love you both, 'til next time,
now off you go!"

BOOKS IN THE SERIES:
QUESTIONS FROM KIDS TO GOD

WHY ARE YOU THAT COLOR?
WHAT IS LOVE?
WHAT IS MY PURPOSE?
WHAT ARE BOUNDARIES?

## About the Author:

Having been raised for a portion of her life in Dominica, Morgan Irby was shown the beauty in simplicity- from bathing in the river behind their house to cutting three holes in a pillowcase and thinking it was the best looking summer dress she'd ever seen. This pursuit of simplicity is seen throughout her words, her illustrations, and her stories. It is her hope that each story transports readers to their own special place where life can be simple again.

# Acknowledgements

Thank you God for allowing me to be a creative vessel for you. I love you so much! I love our relationship, I love learning more about you, and more than anything, I love spending time with you every day.

Thank you Gilliam Writing Group for pairing me with the best writing coach ever - Mariana Roa Oliva!

Thank you Mariana Roa Oliva for being EXACTLY who you are as a person, as a writer, as a coach, as a creative, but most of all as a LIGHT in this world that shines out to the cosmos! The stars look at you and be like, "Yup, she bright, she real bright!!".

Thank you Amy Sowell for being my best friend in the whole world. There is not enough room on this page to thank you for your love and support. To quote Oprah when she spoke about her bestie Gayle, "You are the friend that everybody deserves. I don't know a better person". TRUTH. SLAY QUEEN!

Thank you to my mom for encouraging me throughout this process, for being an example of resilience in a world that can feel hard to navigate sometimes, and thank you for always loving me along the way.

Thank you Marlise Karlin for the energy you bring to this world and ALWAYS reminding me that I have the power to create the life I want.

Thank you Miriam for all your wisdom, guidance, strength, and love. It has shaped me in so many ways. I am forever grateful for your presence in my life. You are a true force in this world!

Thank you Mr. and Mrs. Sowell for seeing me for who I am. It has been the greatest gift! Thank you for all the belly laughs, heartfelt conversations, love, and kindness you have shared with me over the years.

Thank you Irby, Pieratt, and Ingram family for all your love.